HOW TO DRAW
FAST CARS, MONSTER TRUCKS & FIGHTER JETS

CHRISTOPHER HART

WATSON-GUPTILL
PUBLICATIONS
NEW YORK

Dedicated to anyone who has
ever dreamed of owning a Ferrari

Senior Editor: Candace Raney
Project Editor: Alisa Palazzo
Designer: Bob Fillie, Graphiti Design, Inc.
Production Manager: Hector Campbell

Fonts used: Frutiger, Balloon, Bossa Nova

Contributing artists: Grant Meihm, Tom Grindberg, Gray Morrow, Rich Faber

Page 4: The C-5 Galaxy Transport is a cargo transport aircraft used to bring supplies—including munitions, tanks, and troops—to the battlefield. It can lift over 130 tons (260,000 lbs.) of cargo, and requires 4 powerful engines and a fuel tank that takes 51,150 gallons of fuel— enough to fill 6 railroad cars. When empty, it weighs in at 325,244 pounds; filled with cargo, it tilts the scales at three quarters of a million pounds.

First published in 2000 in New York by Watson-Guptill Publications
a division of BPI Communications, Inc.
770 Broadway
New York, NY 10003
www.watsonguptill.com

Library of Congress Cataloging-in-Publication Data
Hart, Christopher.
    How to draw fast cars, monster trucks & fighter jets / Christopher Hart.
        p.   cm.
    Includes index.
    ISBN 0-8230-2395-8
    1. Vehicles in art. 2. Airplanes in art. 3. Drawing—Technique. I. Title.
NC825.V45.H37 2000
743'.89629—dc2   00-033376

Printed in Hong Kong

1 2 3 4 5 6 7 8 / 07 06 05 04 03 02 01 00

www.Hart2Draw.com

SEE YA THERE!

CONTENTS

Introduction 5

Automotive Basics 6

BASIC SHAPES
GENERIC SEDAN BLUEPRINT

HOW A CAR ENGINE WORKS
WHEELS OF FIRE

Ultimate Driving Machines 14

GENERIC SPORTS CAR
FERRARI F 50
LAMBORGHINI COUNTACH
LOTUS ESPRIT
PORSCHE 911 TURBO
DODGE VIPER GTS COUPE

FAST CARS FROM VARIOUS ANGLES
AMERICAN MUSCLE CARS
EVOLUTION OF A THOROUGHBRED: THE FORD MUSTANG
COPS AND ROBBERS
CAR CHASES FROM THE AIR

Collectors Classics 26

1938 BUGATTI ATLANTIC
1954 MERCEDES-BENZ 300SL "GULLWING" COUPE
1957 BMW 507

1961 JAGUAR E-TYPE
1965 ASTON MARTIN DB5
1967 LAMBORGHINI MIURA

Race Cars 32

FORMULA ONE
LE MANS
STOCK CAR

RALLY CROSS
IN THE PIT
WIPE OUT!

Monster Trucks 38

TWO VIEWS OF THE MONSTER TRUCK
CRUSHING CARS

THE CRUSH FROM OVERHEAD
FUNNY CHASSIS

Figher Jets 46

EARLY ATTEMPTS AT FLIGHT
FROM PROPELLERS TO JET ENGINES
HOW A JET ENGINE WORKS
FIGHTER JET BLUEPRINT
F-16 FIGHTING FALCON
F-117A NIGHTHAWK STEALTH FIGHTER
SR-71 BLACKBIRD
TORNADO

F-22 RAPTOR
MiG-29 FULCRUM
A-10 THUNDERBOLT
AH-64D APACHE LONGBOW ATTACK HELICOPTER
L-39C ALBATROSS JET TRAINER
FIGHTER PLANE NOSE DESIGNS
AWACS RADAR PLANE
RQ-3A "DARKSTAR" TIER III MINUS

Index 64

INTRODUCTION

My fascination with sports cars began when I was barely a teenager. My friends and I would ride our bicycles a couple of miles to the exotic-car dealership on the outskirts of town. There we would stare with our mouths agape for hours. I still don't know why the salesmen didn't kick us out. I suppose we were good for business. I remember that I would try to imagine what it would be like to own one of those cars—maybe the Italian convertible or the English roadster or even the German coupe—but I never dared to ask the salesmen if I could actually sit in one. Peaking into the car to steal a glance at the top number on the speedometer gave me a thrill: "Man, 180! Wow!" The thought of those numbers made my head spin. And ever since then, my head always turns to look whenever a Ferrari or a Lamborghini or some other great performance machine cruises past, and I'll bet yours does, too. Even before I tried my hand at cartooning, I was drawing and trying to design sports cars.

This book will show you how to draw all the most exciting, best-known performance vehicles and make them pop right off your page! It's something every comic book artist, illustrator, toy designer, as well as aspiring car designer must know. Plus, you'll learn not only how to draw these cars, but also how they function mechanically—complete with an example of blueprints for a standard body construction and basic engine. This will help you understand how the form of the car follows its function. You'll get car statistics for each one—including engine configuration, maximum power output (horsepower), and top speed—that you can use to get a better feel for each car's strengths, and also to compare the various makes and models.

Then, in addition to the sports cars, there are the monsters. Monster trucks, I mean. If you like monster trucks—and I'm talking about giant trucks with awesome tires that literally crush cars beneath them—then you're definitely in the right place. And, following the monster trucks is a rundown of the most impressive airborne arsenal the world has ever known: the fighter jets of the U.S. Air Force. These crafts are built for amazing speeds. And just as with the sports cars, you'll get all the stats and learn which jets soar to Mach 1, Mach 2, and even Mach 3 (that's 3 times the speed of sound)! You'll discover exactly which weapons these fighters carry on board, from decoys to laser-guided missiles to nukes. Knowing the performance capabilities and payloads of the jets will help you understand the reasons for their particular body designs.

All this and more is right here, waiting for you. So buckle up, lock yourself in, and hold tight, because we're about to put the pedal to the metal!

AUTOMOTIVE BASICS

A good place to start is with Henry Ford, the founder of Ford Motorcars. An industrial visionary, he invented the assembly line, which revolutionized industrial production. Instead of having an entire crew of workers building each car one at a time, from start to finish, Ford had each worker perform only one task, such as installing the steering wheel, while the car was moved from one worker to the next until it was assembled. As a result, cars took less time to build and could therefore be produced and sold for less money. Cars suddenly became affordable to the masses, and paved roads soon followed, as did America's never-ending love affair with the automobile.

Basic Shapes

You can break down a car into a few basic shapes. For our purposes, a car is basically a box—a three-dimensional rectangle. A tire is basically a chopped-off cylinder with a hole in it. In fact, most of the shapes that make up a car, jet, or monster truck are simple, geometric shapes. By breaking down a car into its basic elements, you make the job of drawing it a lot easier. The thing to remember is that all of the shapes that make up a car are three dimensional and, therefore, have both depth and width, as shown here.

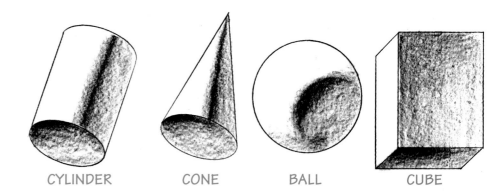

CYLINDER   CONE   BALL   CUBE

Since a tire is circular, to draw one in perspective you can draw an imaginary box as a guide around a cylinder shape and then reduce the cylinder where necessary. Follow the vanishing lines of the boxes, just as you would for rectangular shapes.

A NOTE ABOUT PERSPECTIVE

Drawing things in perspective will give your images a feeling of depth and overall dimension. Shapes drawn in perspective get smaller as they recede into the distance. In order to reduce the right areas of a drawing the right amount, artists use guide-lines, called *vanishing lines,* as shown in the examples here. When positioned correctly, and if extended, these lines should eventually converge at a single *vanishing point* on the horizon. By following correctly placed vanishing lines, you'll be able to draw cars in correct perspective and with correct angles. Most of the illustrations in this book make good use of vanishing lines, so don't worry if it sounds complicated at first; by following the steps on each page, you'll be learning how to draw in perspective.

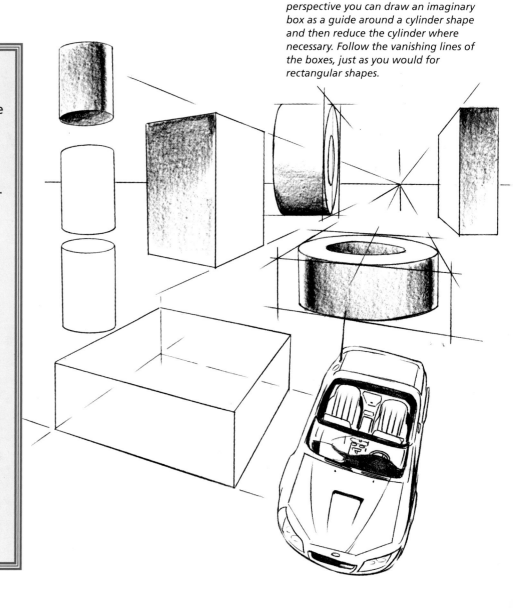

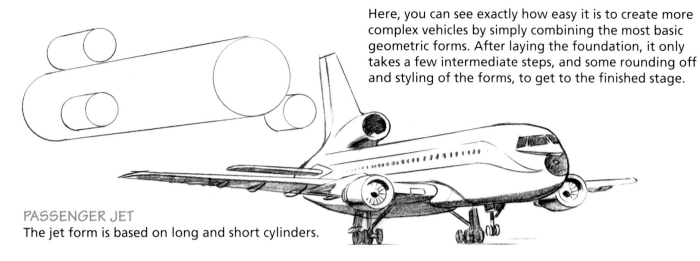

Here, you can see exactly how easy it is to create more complex vehicles by simply combining the most basic geometric forms. After laying the foundation, it only takes a few intermediate steps, and some rounding off and styling of the forms, to get to the finished stage.

PASSENGER JET
The jet form is based on long and short cylinders.

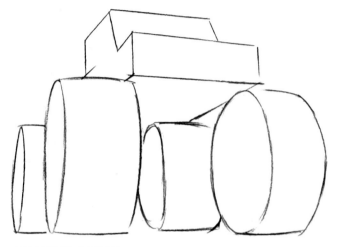

MONSTER TRUCK
The truck body is two rectangles stacked one on top of the other. The tires are truncated cylinders.

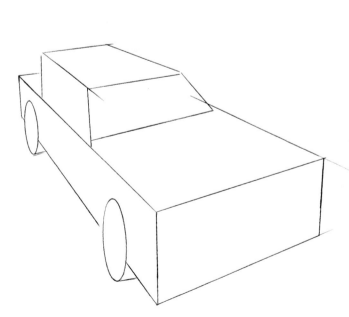

SPORTS CAR
Similar to the truck, the sports car is also basically two rectangles stacked one on top of the other, with some rounding off of the windshield, indicating its forward slope. And again, the tires are nothing more than truncated cylinders.

Generic Sedan Blueprint

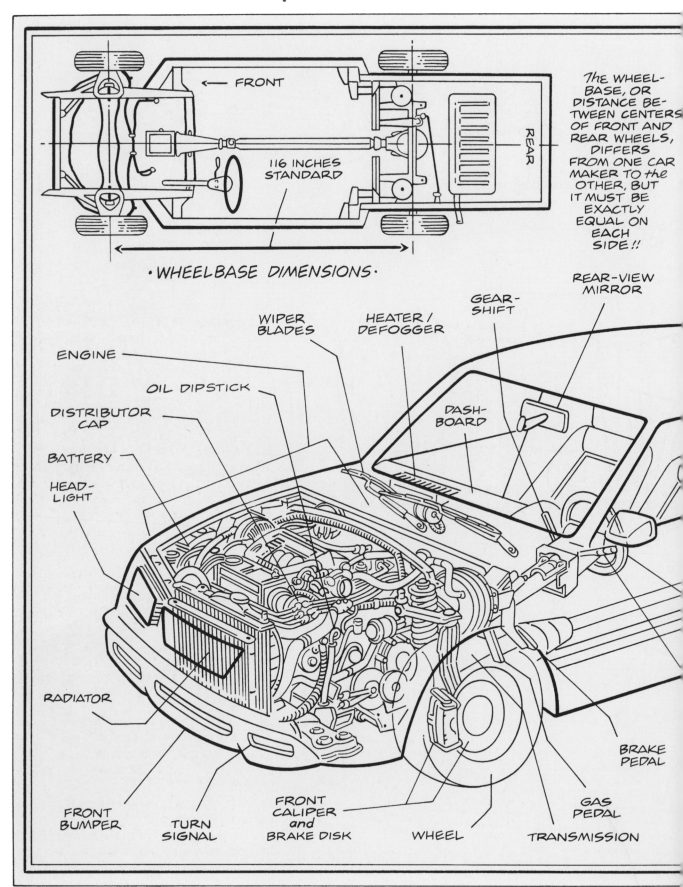

FRONT ←

116 INCHES STANDARD

REAR

The WHEEL-BASE, OR DISTANCE BE-TWEEN CENTERS OF FRONT AND REAR WHEELS, DIFFERS FROM ONE CAR MAKER TO the OTHER, BUT IT MUST BE EXACTLY EQUAL ON EACH SIDE !!

· WHEELBASE DIMENSIONS ·

REAR-VIEW MIRROR

GEAR-SHIFT

HEATER / DEFOGGER

WIPER BLADES

ENGINE

OIL DIPSTICK

DASH-BOARD

DISTRIBUTOR CAP

BATTERY

HEAD-LIGHT

RADIATOR

FRONT BUMPER

TURN SIGNAL

FRONT CALIPER and BRAKE DISK

WHEEL

TRANSMISSION

GAS PEDAL

BRAKE PEDAL

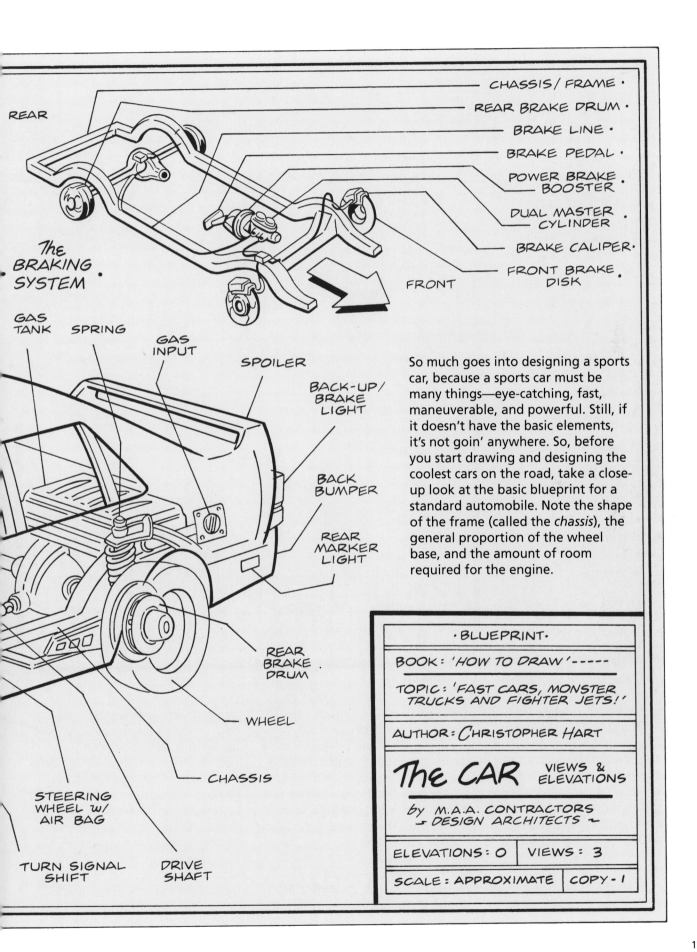

REAR

CHASSIS / FRAME ·

REAR BRAKE DRUM ·

BRAKE LINE ·

BRAKE PEDAL ·

POWER BRAKE BOOSTER ·

DUAL MASTER CYLINDER ·

BRAKE CALIPER ·

FRONT BRAKE DISK ·

FRONT

The BRAKING SYSTEM ·

GAS TANK

SPRING

GAS INPUT

SPOILER

BACK-UP/ BRAKE LIGHT

BACK BUMPER

REAR MARKER LIGHT

REAR BRAKE DRUM

WHEEL

CHASSIS

STEERING WHEEL w/ AIR BAG

TURN SIGNAL SHIFT

DRIVE SHAFT

So much goes into designing a sports car, because a sports car must be many things—eye-catching, fast, maneuverable, and powerful. Still, if it doesn't have the basic elements, it's not goin' anywhere. So, before you start drawing and designing the coolest cars on the road, take a close-up look at the basic blueprint for a standard automobile. Note the shape of the frame (called the *chassis*), the general proportion of the wheel base, and the amount of room required for the engine.

· BLUEPRINT ·	
BOOK: 'HOW TO DRAW'-----	
TOPIC: 'FAST CARS, MONSTER TRUCKS AND FIGHTER JETS!'	
AUTHOR: CHRISTOPHER HART	
The CAR VIEWS & ELEVATIONS	
by M.A.A. CONTRACTORS ~ DESIGN ARCHITECTS ~	
ELEVATIONS: O	VIEWS: 3
SCALE: APPROXIMATE	COPY - 1

How a Car Engine Works

A car engine is an internal combustion engine. Combustion is the occurrence of burning, and the combustion engine is so called because it burns a mixture of gasoline and air, which generates energy that can be used to create motion. The top diagram identifies the main engine parts, while the bottom diagram explains how the engine actually works.

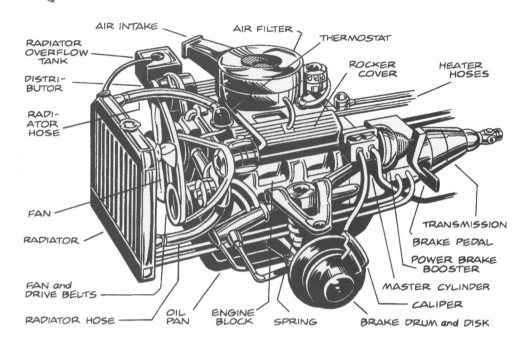

THE 4-STROKE COMBUSTION CYCLE AND ENGINE CONFIGURATIONS

Most current cars use a 4-stroke combustion cycle to convert gasoline into energy and motion. Here's how it works. As the intake valve on top of a cylinder opens, the crankshaft rotates, pulling the connecting rod and the attached piston down to let air and gasoline into the cylinder (1). The rotation of the crankshaft continues, moving the piston all the way down and then back up to compress the air-and-fuel mixture (2), and when the piston reaches the top of the cylinder, the spark plug emits a spark to ignite the gasoline (3). The charge in the cylinder explodes, forcing the piston down, and once the piston reaches the bottom of the cylinder, the exhaust valve opens and the exhaust leaves the cylinder (4), setting the car in motion and exiting from the car's tailpipe. The cycle then begins again and is repeated over and over.

Most cars have multiple-cylinder engines; 4, 6, and 8 cylinders are

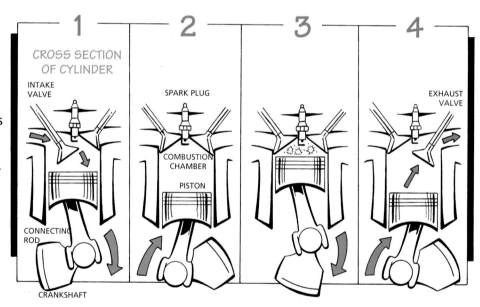

common, and some sports cars have 10 or even 12. Generally speaking, the more cylinders, the larger the engine—and, therefore, the longer the section of the car that houses the engine (either the front or the back, depending on the model). The cylinders are usually arranged in one of 3 configurations, whichever is most suitable for the vehicle: in-line or straight (cylinders in a line, one after the other); V (cylinders at a V-shaped

angle to one another, and the degree of the angle can vary from car to car); and horizontally opposed or flat (cylinders lie opposite one another and flat in the same plane, with no V angle). The notation V-4, for example, indicates that an engine has 4 cylinders arranged in a V configuration; V-8 indicates 8 cylinders in a V configuration, and so on. Flat 6 indicates 6 cylinders in a horizontally opposed/flat configuration.

Wheels of Fire

Many less-experienced artists often work hard to make the car bodies look great but never focus on the wheels. It's just 4 circles, they think. Well, not exactly. Unless the car is completely in profile, the wheels are going to have some volume and depth. The treads will show, or at least there should be some streaks where the rubber hits the road. Don't draw the wheels too thin, especially on sports cars, which typically have fatter tires to better grip the road when executing sharp turns. And, on monster trucks, the knobby tire treads should be huge!

FAMILY CAR

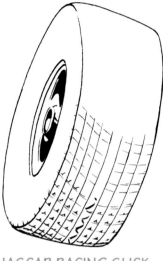

NASCAR RACING SLICK

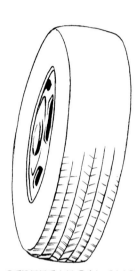

STREET LEGAL SLICK

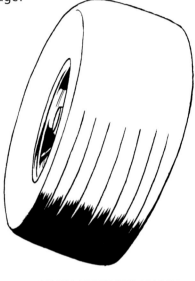

HIGH PERFORMANCE

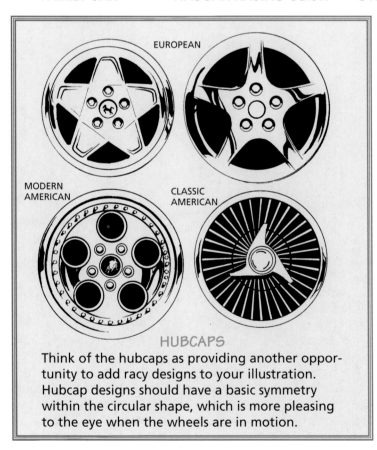

EUROPEAN

MODERN AMERICAN

CLASSIC AMERICAN

HUBCAPS

Think of the hubcaps as providing another opportunity to add racy designs to your illustration. Hubcap designs should have a basic symmetry within the circular shape, which is more pleasing to the eye when the wheels are in motion.

MONSTER TRUCK

ULTIMATE DRIVING MACHINES

L ife's not fair. You spend much of your youth pining for an expensive, exotic sports car. But, by the time you can actually afford one, you're wearing a hairpiece and having touble getting your seat belt around your stomach.

Generic Sports Car

Before attempting to draw a specific car model, it's a good idea to familiarize yourself with the basic characteristics of the sports car. In general, nothing juts out from the body that could create wind resistance; even the passenger cabin is quite shallow so that air travels easily over the car. There's often a spoiler in back to force the air current to press down on the rear end of the vehicle when the car reaches speeds in excess of 100 mph (miles per hour); without the spoiler, the rear end would tend to lift off the ground when it hits bumps and be less stable in general at high speeds.

Of course each high-performance vehicle has its own unique angles and shapes that you must capture in your drawings, in order to create a representation that is immediately recognizable as that particular make and model. But, mastering the general features mentioned above will ensure that your drawings read clearly as sports cars.

When drawing a frontal shot like this one, shorten the length of the rear end of the car, because it's farther away from you (see information on perspective on page 8).

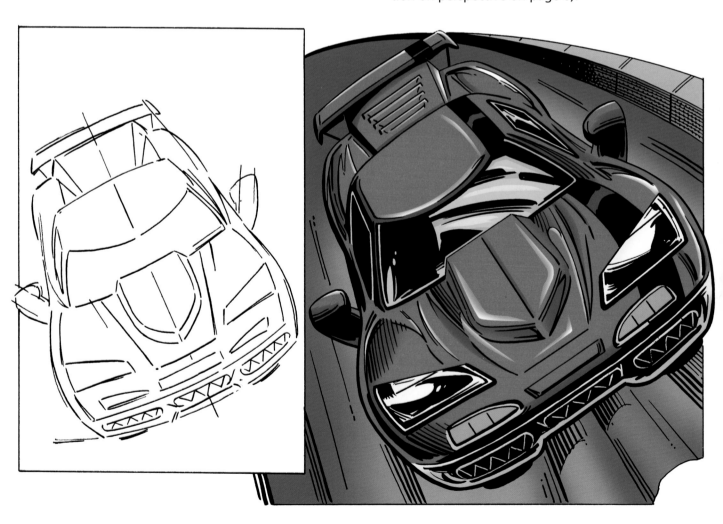

Ferrari F 50

Just the name Ferrari summons up excitement and dreams of speed. The company was founded by Enzo Ferrari (1898-1988), who spent much of the early part of his career as a test and race driver at Alfa Romeo, ultimately becoming director of the Alfa racing division. Design and production on the very first Ferrari began in 1946, and Ferraris got their reputation by winning races. From these victories, the company moved to producing sports cars with cutting-edge performance. Always stylish, with unmistakable Italian charisma, Ferraris maintain a look of defiant power channeled into a precision driving machine.

When drawing a sports car, try to think in terms of descriptive adjectives (or nouns) for your illustration, to help you visualize the look you're trying to attain. For Ferraris, the words that come to my mind are "aggressive," "stylish," "flair," and "fast."

Note the high-back bucket seats.

STATS:

ENGINE: V-12

MAX. POWER OUTPUT:
  513 horsepower

TOP SPEED: 202 mph

0–60 MPH: 3.7 seconds

Lamborghini Countach

Not only do Italians make the best food and the most stylish clothes, but they're not too shabby when it comes to making world-class sports cars either. Enter the Lamborghini Countach. Ah, if I told you how many times I dreamed of owning one of these babies when I was a teenager. . . . Oh well, at least we can draw, can't we? How about that takeoff on the "gullwing" door (see page 27)? Instead of opening like regular car doors, these open vertically, pivoting upward from the forward-most point on the door. And look at how the hood dips down like the nose on a fighter jet! Produced through the late '80s, this is the kind of car that stops pedestrians in their tracks. I don't know if anyone has ever gotten a speeding ticket driving one—all the highway patrol sees is a cloud of dust in the Lamborghini's wake. Adjectives that come to my mind for this model are "exotic," "outrageous," "sleek," and "cool."

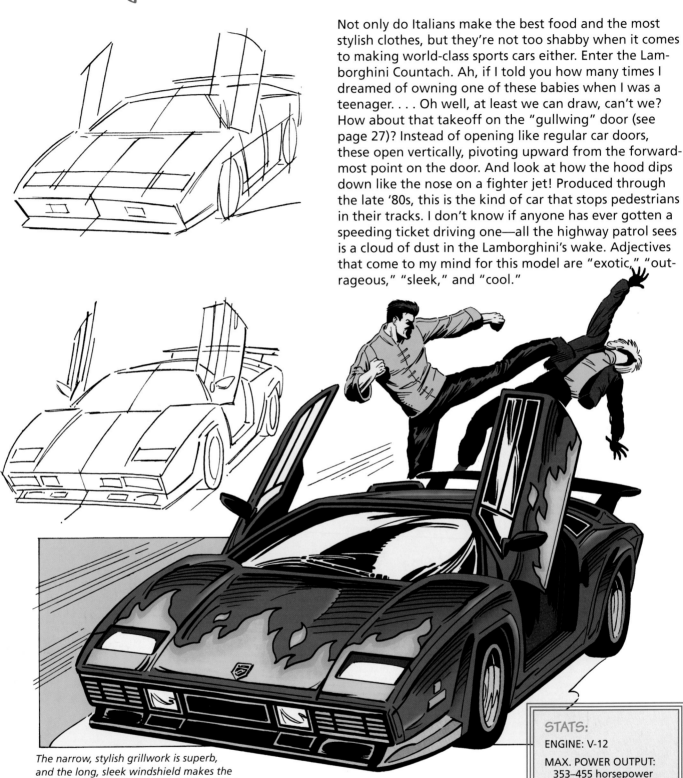

The narrow, stylish grillwork is superb, and the long, sleek windshield makes the Countach an eye-catcher from any angle.

Note that the mirrors are attached to the doors, not to the front end of the body.

STATS:

ENGINE: V-12

MAX. POWER OUTPUT: 353–455 horsepower (depending on model)

TOP SPEED: 177–195 mph (depending on model)

0–60 MPH: 3.9 seconds (may vary with model)

Lotus Esprit

One of the great exotic cars of all time, the British-made Lotus Esprit combines grace and style with raw, rugged power. Able to zoom from 0 to 60 mph in under 4½ seconds, it can suck the doors off much of the competition, and the 5-speed manual transmission makes it a dream car for performance enthusiasts. The Lotus has been featured in many action movies, including the James Bond film *The Spy Who Loved Me,* in which it functioned both as land vehicle and submarine (courtesy a separate car that was modified to go underwater). It's no accident that high-end, exotic sports cars appear in action movies: These cars appeal to the teenager in all of us.

STATS:

ENGINE: V-8

MAX. POWER OUTPUT:
  350 horsepower

TOP SPEED: approx. 175 mph

0–62 MPH: 4.7 seconds

0–100 MPH: 10.2 seconds

The Lotus Esprit is beautifully proportioned, with a sleek, extended front end that's low to the ground and thick tires to grip the road for quick maneuvering.

Porsche 911 Turbo

Admit it. You want this baby. The Porsche 911 traces its design back to the Porsche roadsters of the 1960s. German-designed and -built, it is characterized by a protruding front end, compact passenger compartment, and small rear end, often with a spoiler. (See page 20 for rear view.) The superfast, super-handling 911 Turbo is built for a driver's driver—someone who longs to feel the road beneath the car. If you want to know if it comes with an automatic transmission, rather than a manual one, you probably shouldn't own it. Top speed is 189 mph. Hold on to your toupees, all you rich guys.

STATS:

ENGINE: Flat 6 (rear-mounted)

MAX. POWER OUTPUT:
414 horsepower

TOP SPEED: 189 mph

0–62 MPH: 4.4 seconds

Make sure the roof is dome shaped, and never forget the hefty spoiler in the back. Also, always include those stylish Porsche headlights that wrap around the sides of the car.

Dodge Viper GTS Coupe

If you're looking for an American answer to all the foreign sports cars, look no further than the Dodge Viper. (Also see page 20 for another view.) With a V-10 engine pumping out 450 horses and a top speed of 200 mph, the Viper isn't just messing around. Yet it has retained its decidedly American look of simplicity coupled with strength. And . . . it's a steal for under $100,000! Priced so that even a moderately wealthy person can afford one.

STATS:

ENGINE: V-10

MAX. POWER OUTPUT:
  450 horsepower

TOP SPEED: 200 mph

0-60 MPH: approx. 4.8 seconds

Note the long, rounded front end, as compared with the thinner, wedge-shaped fronts of many foreign high-performance vehicles. The large front end is typical American muscle in an ultramodern design. Also, the passenger cabin here is higher than the sloping designs of many comparable foreign cars.

Evolution of a Thoroughbred: The Ford Mustang

The Ford Mustang is arguably the most enduring name in American sports cars. Reasonably priced when it first hit the market, the Mustang became an instant hit and, decades later, a certifiable classic car, selling for many times its original price.

All cars go through design changes. It's an important way to keep customers interested in the brand and to evolve with consumer trends. Ford started off the Mustang with a zippy, sexy design and soon began beefing up its engine size, horsepower, and tire sizes with truly awesome results. However, by the time the Mach 1 Mustang rolled out in the 1970s, the car was huge and, in my opinion, more boatlike than sleek.

Ford then regrouped and came out with a newly designed Mustang II, which was affordable but lacked any pretense of being a true sports car. Still you have to hand it to Ford, because the company just wouldn't put this noble stallion out to pasture. Back to the tool shed it went once more, but this time with the spirit of the original firmly in mind.

The Mustangs of the 1980s roared into showrooms. These true sports cars had muscle and style at affordable prices. Mustang had gotten its act together again, and they keep getting better in each successive decade. It's an amazing history, with highs and lows—but without a doubt, the thoroughbred is back.

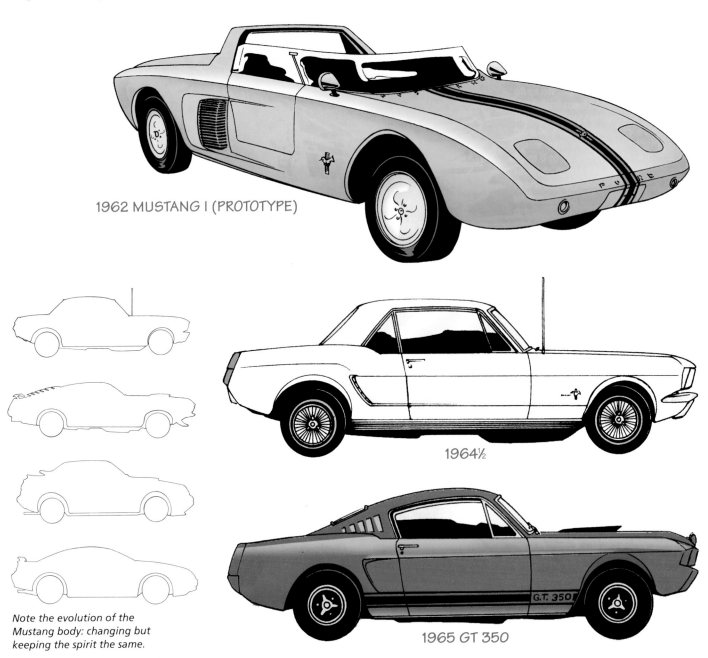

1962 MUSTANG I (PROTOTYPE)

1964½

1965 GT 350

Note the evolution of the Mustang body: changing but keeping the spirit the same.

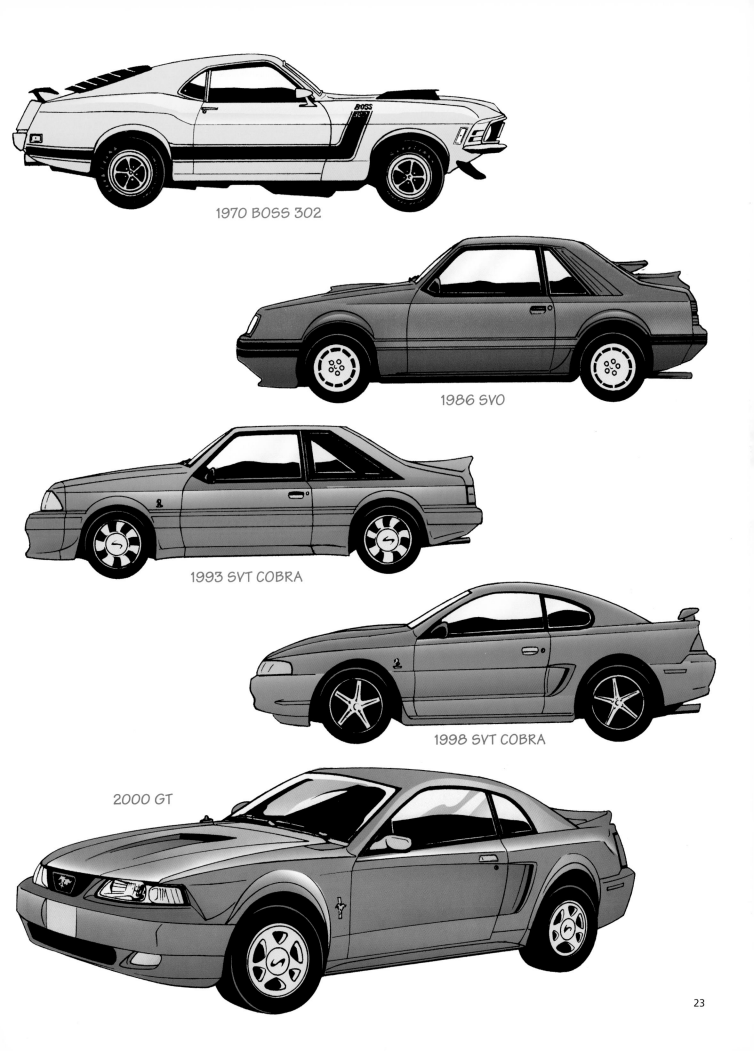

1970 BOSS 302

1986 SVO

1993 SVT COBRA

1998 SVT COBRA

2000 GT

Cops and Robbers

What would a comic book or a megabucks Hollywood movie be without a car chase? If you want to have a hot chase scene, you need somebody in hot pursuit—and that's usually a cop. While the markings and colors on police cars change from time to time, and also vary from state to state, the classic black-and-white cop car is always easily recognizable as such. A typical police car paint job has white on the passenger cabin, white on the front doors, and black everywhere else. "Black and whites" are almost always domestic sedans. They have a screen guard between the back seat, where the criminals are held, and the front seat, where the cops sit. The cop car shown here is a Ford Crown Victoria, and the car eluding it is a Viper . . . heh, heh. Don't bet on the law.

Car Chases from the Air

Okay, so you've outrun the heat. You're free and clear, right? Wrong! Here come the Feds (Federal law enforcement agents) in choppers, pursuing you from the air. What's a fleeing, falsely-accused gal-set-up-to-take-the-fall-for-a-corrupt-public-official supposed to do? Shoot at the propellers of course! In every good chase scene with multiple pursuers, the guy or gal being pursued takes out a bunch of the would be captors in the process, balancing out the odds and providing lots of splashy explosions and crashes. And by the by, that's a Ford Mustang Cobra being chased by two Hughes 500 helicopters. Advantage choppers.

COLLECTORS CLASSICS

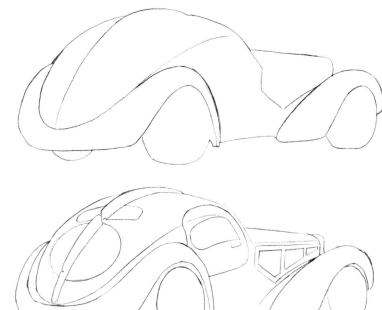

It can happen to anyone. You hit the lottery, wind up with 70 or 80 million bucks, get soaked for a few million by your leechlike relatives, and still have more money than you know what to do with. But be frustrated no more! You are just the type of person who should be collecting classic cars. They cost a fortune, they're beautiful, and totally impractical. So, here's your basic classic car shopping list.

1938 Bugatti Atlantic

One of the rarest and most prestigious cars in the world is, predictably, Italian-designed. The designer of the Atlantic was Jean Bugatti, son of Ettore Bugatti who began the famous line of what are now museum-quality cars. The Bugattis came from a long line of artists and artisans, and boy, does it show. The Atlantic has the sweeping lines and curves of a luxury car but the posture and grit of a roadster, bearing out the fact that Ettore Bugatti earned his fame the old fashioned way: He won a lot of races.

1954 Mercedes-Benz 300SL "Gullwing" Coupe

The pinnacle of Mercedes-Benz classics, the Gullwing is a beauty to behold. It got its nickname because its doors, which opened upward, reminded people of seagull wings. Debuting in 1952 as a racing car that blew the competition away, the Gullwing was put into mass production in 1954. And lest you think it's simply a pretty car from yesteryear, take a look at that Stats box. Not bad for a car designed in 1954, eh?

STATS:

ENGINE: 6 cylinders

MAX. POWER OUTPUT: 300 horsepower

TOP SPEED: about 150 mph

1957 BMW 507

The 507 Beemer is considered by many to be the most beautiful car of all time. No, it's not the fastest car, with top speeds of only 118 to 136 mph—but the elegant lines of this roadster are hard to match. Note the sweeping curve that travels from the headlight to the door; the beautiful, subtle shape of the hood; and that classic BMW grillwork. The car's form is expertly balanced: The rear fin glides gently over the rear wheel and blends into the door, creating a rear section that matches the front end to perfection. And it's a ragtop to boot!

INTERESTING
507 FACT
Total BMW 507 production ran from 1956 to 1959, and only 254 were built—all virtually by hand.

STATS:
ENGINE: V-8

MAX. POWER OUTPUT:
   150 horsepower

TOP SPEED: 118–136 mph
   (depending on rear axle)

1961 Jaguar E-Type

Oh, what a feeling to gaze upon perfection in metal. The Jaguar E-Type is, in my humble opinion, the most beautiful car ever built. And although it's fast, it is also, to put it mildly, a challenge to keep out of the repair shop, as has been reported to me by various car buffs. (Jags gained a solid reputation for dependability when Ford took over the company.) But when you're this pretty, who can complain about a few repair bills?

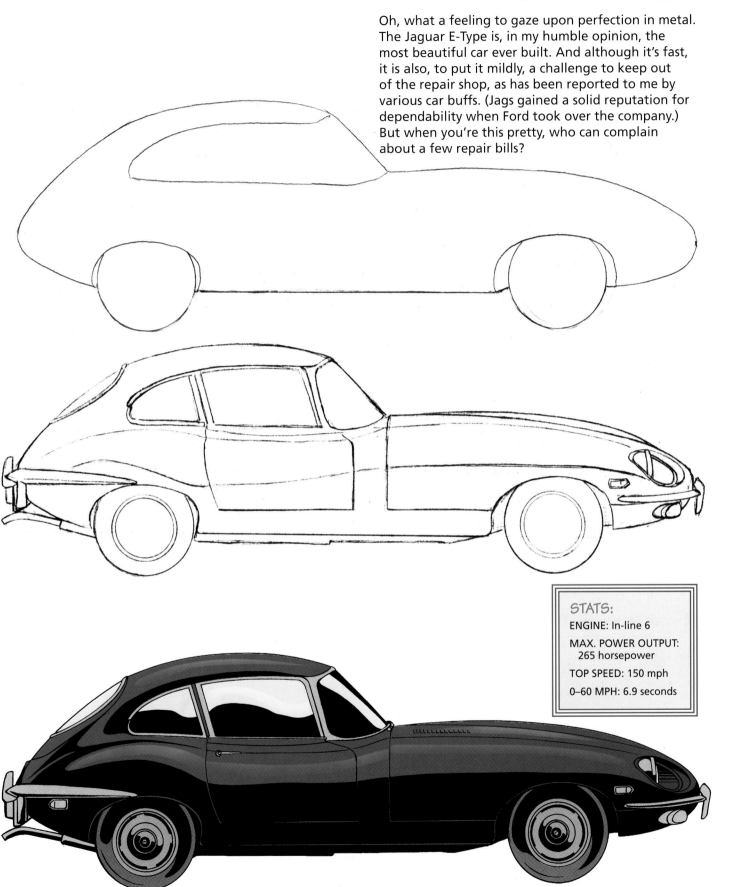

STATS:

ENGINE: In-line 6

MAX. POWER OUTPUT: 265 horsepower

TOP SPEED: 150 mph

0–60 MPH: 6.9 seconds

29

1965 Aston Martin DB5

Who wouldn't love to have the car that Sean Connery's James Bond made famous first in *Goldfinger* and then in *Thunderball*? This is an ultracool sports car with class. You'll notice that these later classic sports cars look sleeker than the earlier models, owing to more efficient aerodynamic designs. Unfortunately, only about 1,000 DB5 units were made, and of those, only 65 had the special, high-performance Vantage engine, which increased horsepower. Still, with a 6-cylinder engine, it nonetheless powered to a top speed of 140 mph. Take that, Mr. Bond.

MAXIMUM POWER OUTPUT:
THE VANTAGE ADVANTAGE

WITHOUT VANTAGE:
282 horsepower

WITH VANTAGE:
325 horsepower

1967 Lamborghini Miura

Lamborghini just doesn't know how to make an ugly car. Every model seems destined to be a classic, and the Miura was no exception. Exquisite, sleek lines, a wedge-shaped front end, and a sloping rear window are the hallmarks of this gem. It was the first production car in the world to use a centrally mounted engine, which gives excellent stability. This revolutionary mid-engine design, powered by a V-12, hits a top speed of close to 170 mph. Not too shabby.

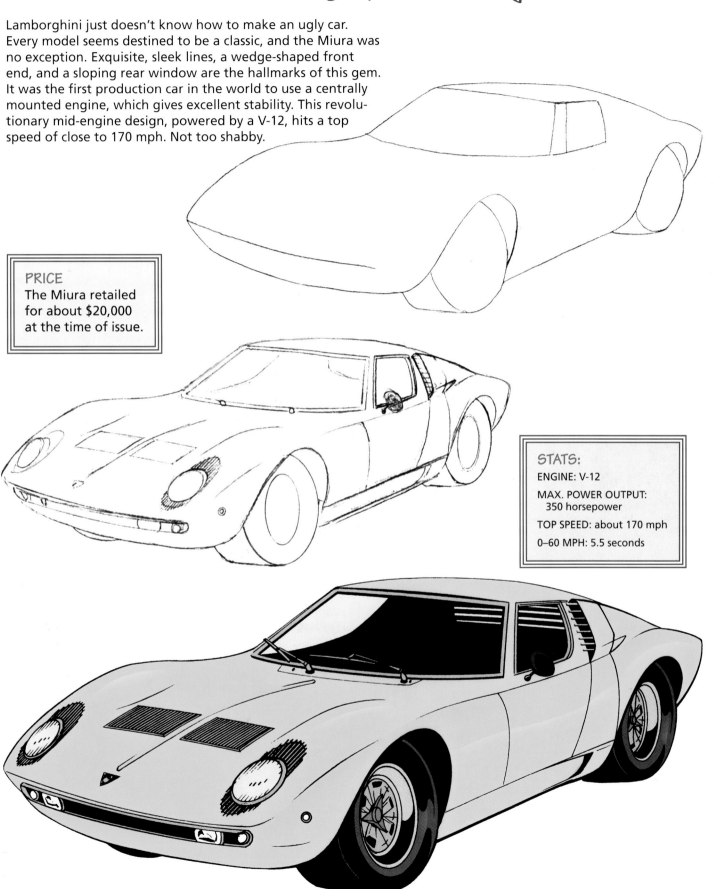

PRICE
The Miura retailed for about $20,000 at the time of issue.

STATS:

ENGINE: V-12

MAX. POWER OUTPUT:
350 horsepower

TOP SPEED: about 170 mph

0–60 MPH: 5.5 seconds

RACE CARS

C ar racing is one of the biggest spectator sports in the world. Races command devoted fans and heavy television coverage. As there isn't just one type of race, there isn't just one specific type of race car—the models are designed to be track specific. Each race course requires a special breed of race car.

Formula One

The Formula One cars are built for street race courses, such as the famous Monte Carlo Street Circuit in Monaco. Speeds average from 120 to 180 mph, but the cars must be able to slow down to 40 mph in a heartbeat to avoid wiping out around hairpin turns. Formula One cars are noted for their extremely wide, exposed tires; single seat; and narrow body design. Note the heavy use of vanishing lines in the preliminary drawing; using guidelines like this is often a good idea.

Le Mans

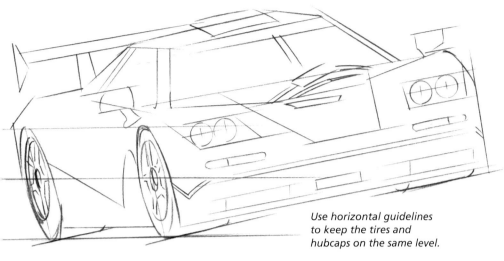

Le Mans race cars are made from exotic car bodies—which are plenty fast to begin with—and are then customized to the specifications of the track. The result: very low and wide cars, offering little wind resistance to slow them down. The Le Mans race in France has the highest profile of all the Le Mans events. It's a grueling, 24-hour endurance race in which the cars are pushed to the limit and then some. Breakdowns are heartbreakingly common and can sideline even drivers who have come within striking distance of winning the race.

This 3/4 view foreshortens the car, making it appear more compact—as if viewed through a telephoto lens. It's a favored angle among car illustrators, because it shows the dramatic front end, as well as some of both the front and rear wheels.

Use horizontal guidelines to keep the tires and hubcaps on the same level.

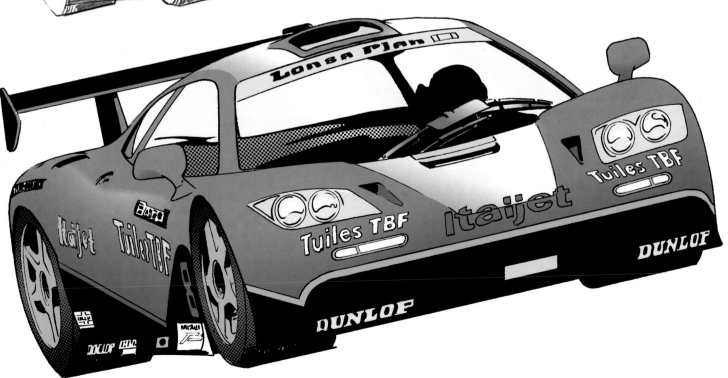

Stock Car

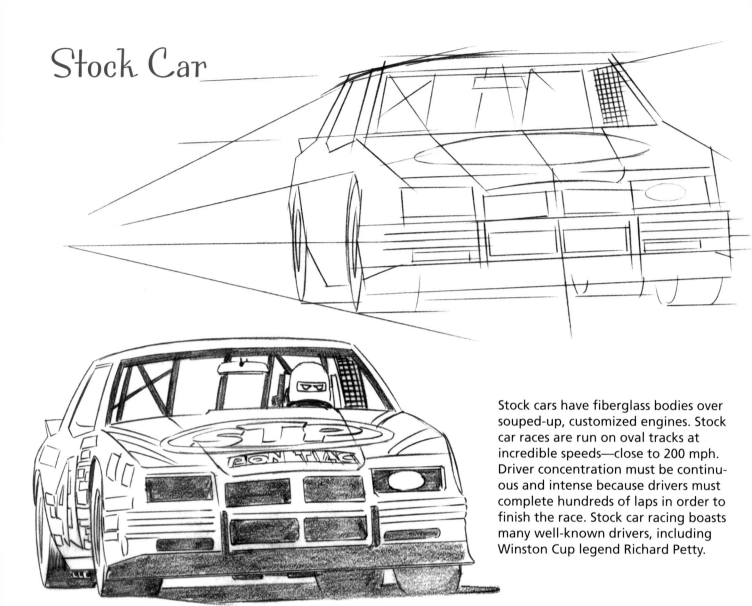

Stock cars have fiberglass bodies over souped-up, customized engines. Stock car races are run on oval tracks at incredible speeds—close to 200 mph. Driver concentration must be continuous and intense because drivers must complete hundreds of laps in order to finish the race. Stock car racing boasts many well-known drivers, including Winston Cup legend Richard Petty.

Note the use of darker tones inside the car, as well as below the chassis, to indicate shadows where the overhead sunlight cannot penetrate.

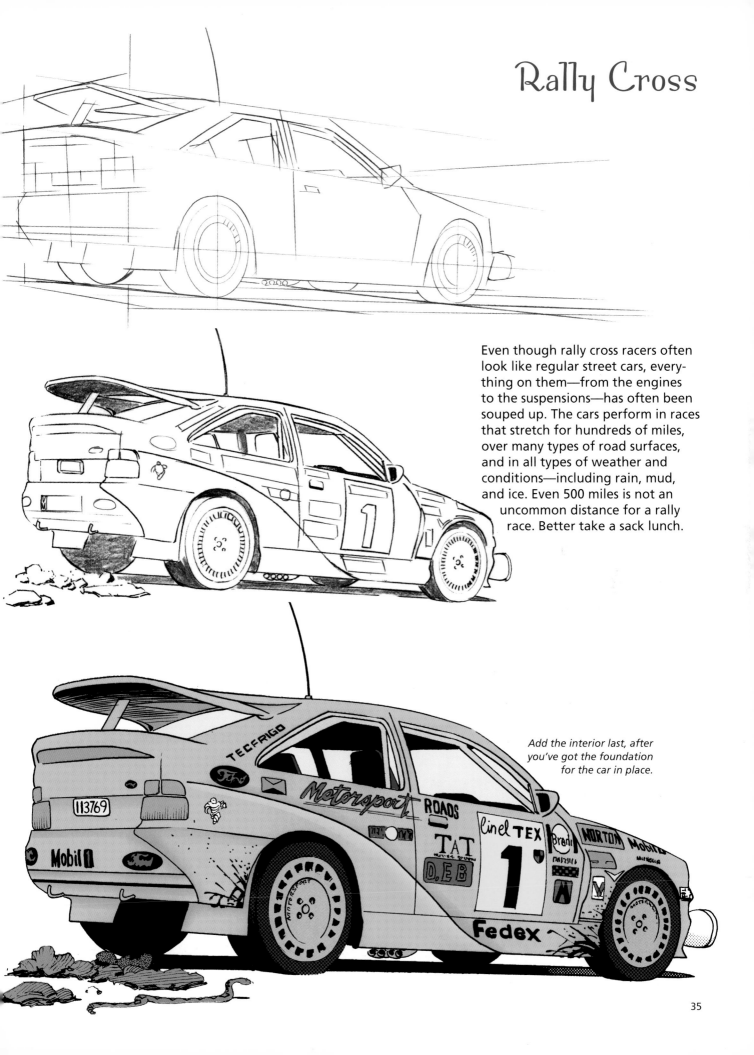

Even though rally cross racers often look like regular street cars, everything on them—from the engines to the suspensions—has often been souped up. The cars perform in races that stretch for hundreds of miles, over many types of road surfaces, and in all types of weather and conditions—including rain, mud, and ice. Even 500 miles is not an uncommon distance for a rally race. Better take a sack lunch.

Add the interior last, after you've got the foundation for the car in place.

35

In the Pit

The pit crew (here a stock car pit crew) is almost as important as the driver. It's the driver's lifeblood. If the car isn't performing exactly right, the ones in the pit are the doctors who have·to diagnose the problem and solve it at lightning speed. Within the pit crew there's a distinct hierarchy, with the more experienced members directing the repairs.

Note, when drawing crowd scenes, that you don't have to delineate hundreds of individual figures. Just a rough spattering of ink or some lines suggesting the people will do.

Wipe Out!

Accidents are part of the dangerous world of auto racing. They hold a grim fascination for spectators because they're undeniably compelling spectacles. Who hasn't been mesmerized by a wicked crash in which the driver survives, unharmed? Television news programs play crash footage over and over, in slow motion and from as many angles as possible. The cars are going at such outrageous speeds that they frequently launch into the air and flip over, breaking apart as they career toward a barrier wall.

MONSTER TRUCKS

Okay, all you steak-eaters, here's some more red meat for you: crushing, bruising, cruising monster trucks. They ain't polite, and they ain't pretty—but they're trouble for anyone or anything that gets in their way!

RACING

Two Views of the Monster Truck

3/4 FRONT LEFT

Unlike a sports car, which is low to the ground, the monster truck is a giant. So this means that you're going to be looking up at it and seeing some of its underbelly. Form the tires from extra-wide cylinders, and be sure to overlap them; here the truck's front left tire overlaps its back ones. Get the positioning of the tires right first, before drawing the treads—and be sure all the treads on all the tires are traveling in the same direction! The chassis rests way above the tires so that the tires don't hit the wheel well when the truck rolls over a high obstacle.

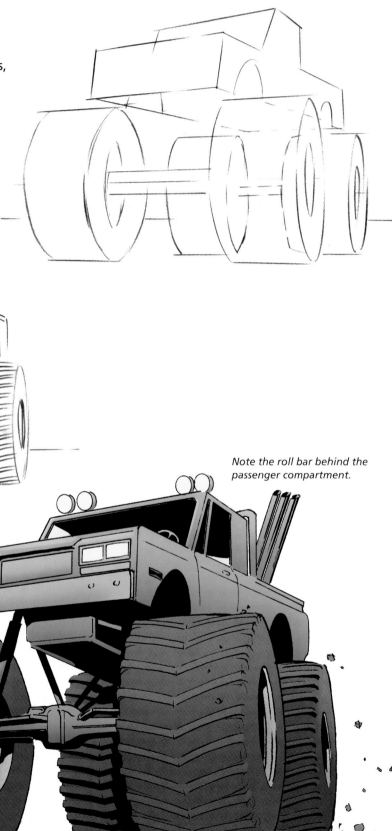

Note the roll bar behind the passenger compartment.

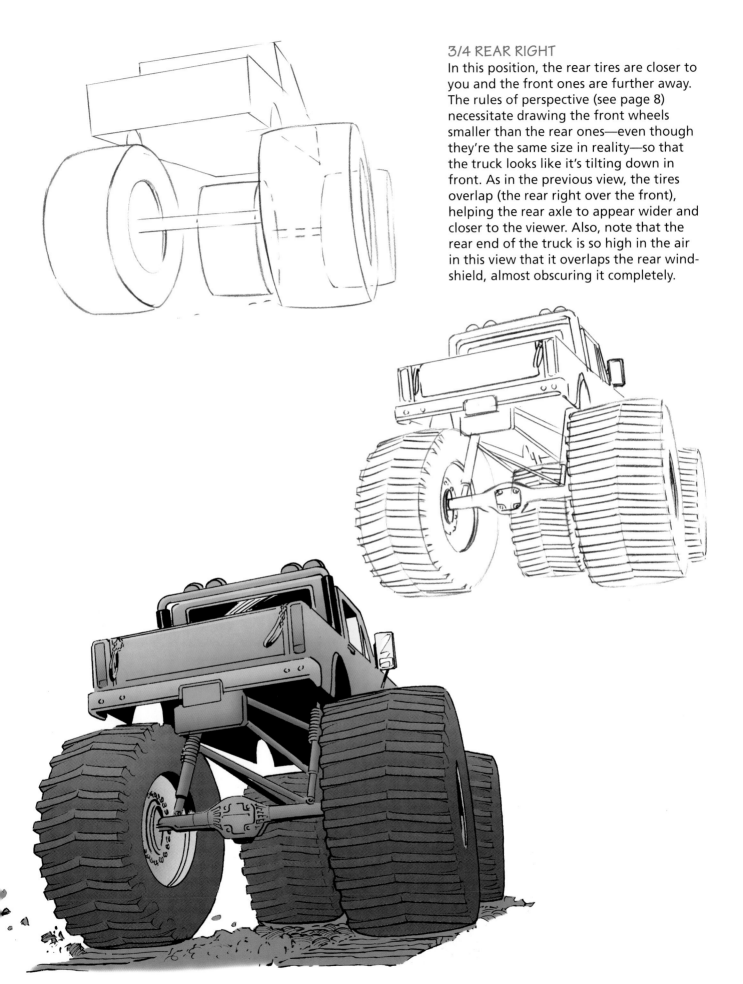

3/4 REAR RIGHT

In this position, the rear tires are closer to you and the front ones are further away. The rules of perspective (see page 8) necessitate drawing the front wheels smaller than the rear ones—even though they're the same size in reality—so that the truck looks like it's tilting down in front. As in the previous view, the tires overlap (the rear right over the front), helping the rear axle to appear wider and closer to the viewer. Also, note that the rear end of the truck is so high in the air in this view that it overlaps the rear windshield, almost obscuring it completely.

Crushing Cars

3/4 FRONT RIGHT

You expect a monster truck to go
for a nice, leisurely drive down Main Street? Au
contraire, pal. What's life for, if not to crush a
couple of cars along the way? Note that monster
trucks can lift way up on their front tires, and
when those rear tires fall back down again,
they'll add a second smasharoo to the cars.

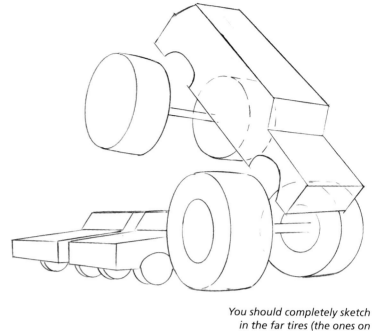

*You should completely sketch
in the far tires (the ones on
the left side of the car here),
even though they'll be mostly
blocked from view in the
finished drawing. This will
help you with your placement.*

A NOTE ABOUT PAINT JOBS

Many folks lovingly detail their trucks. This good ol' boy has gone and put a pair of longhorns on the hood and a tail on the rear end. Once a cowboy, always a cowboy.

Be sure to show metal debris in the air, coming from underneath the truck tires.

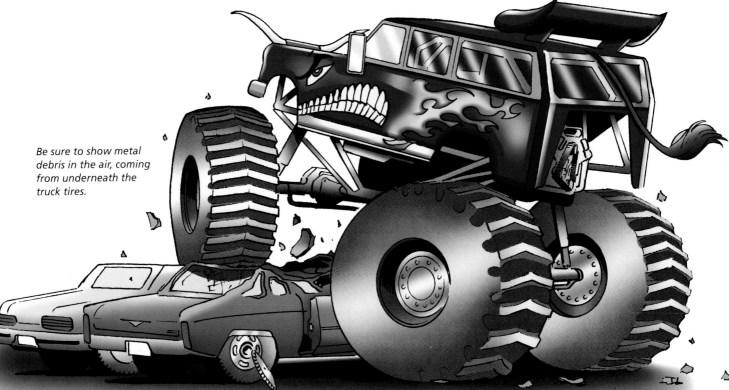

The Crush from Overhead

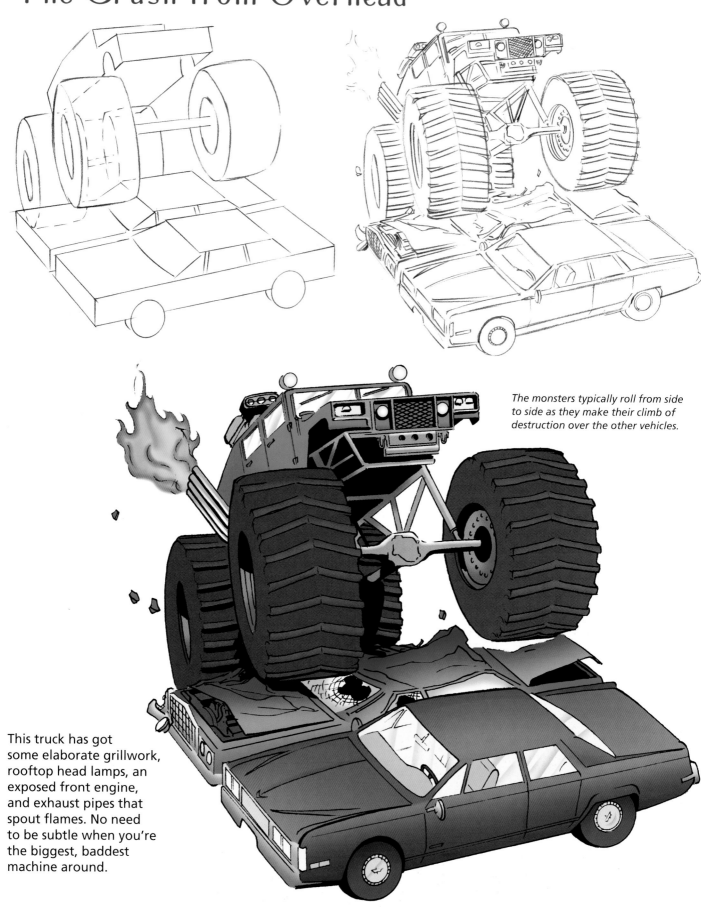

The monsters typically roll from side to side as they make their climb of destruction over the other vehicles.

This truck has got some elaborate grillwork, rooftop head lamps, an exposed front engine, and exhaust pipes that spout flames. No need to be subtle when you're the biggest, baddest machine around.

Funny Chassis

Monster trucks can have any style truck body. How about a hearse? Sort of gets the point across that this truck isn't gonna take any prisoners.

FIGHTER JETS

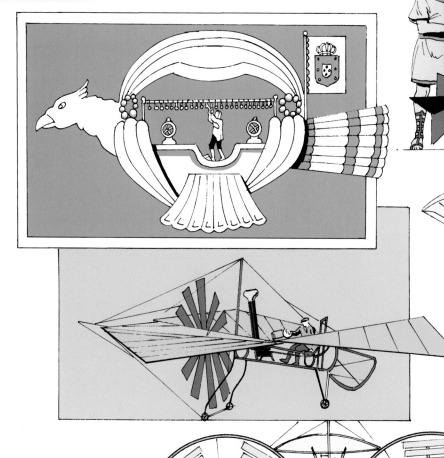

Ever since he first saw birds soaring overhead, man has been fascinated by the possibilities of flight. Without much more than lumber, some simple tools, and a complete ignorance of the principles of aerodynamics, man set in motion one of his greatest victories—the conquest of the skies. However, like all great victories, this one had humble origins that were often as humorous as they were humiliating!

Early Attempts at Flight

All of the machines pictured here carried with them great hopes for success, but all met with dismal failure. When you see today's high-tech fighter jets, it's hard to believe that anyone once thought these earliest contraptions would actually fly.

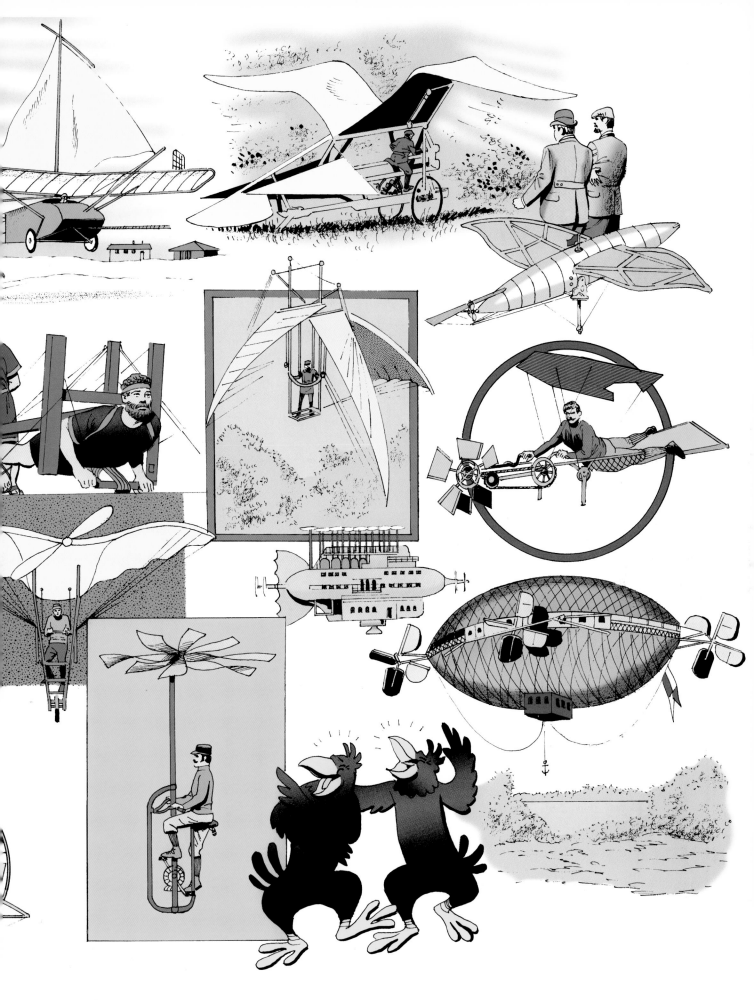

From Propellers to Jet Engines

There were no jet fighters through World War II. It wasn't until the Korean War in the 1950s that fighter aircraft acquired the powerful jet engines that would rocket modern pilots to previously undreamt of speeds and levels of maneuverability. Unlike propellers, jet engines use air to burn fuel and create motion. This momentous engine transformation also required a complete redesigning and streamlining of the aircraft themselves. Modern fighter jets would eventually make maximum use of aerodynamics, offer night and all-weather vision, and be capable of carrying significant payloads of bombs, laser-guided missiles, and decoys.

How a Jet Engine Works

The jet engine is designed to force cool air into a chamber, where it mixes with ignited fuel, resulting in expanding, fast moving, hot gases. The high-speed rush of these gases spins the turbine (a rotating spindle in the center of the engine), providing maximum power to the fighter craft.

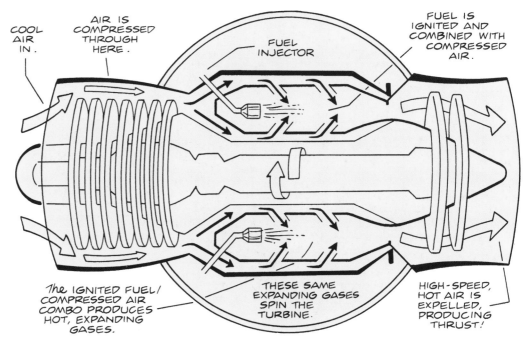

COOL AIR IN.

AIR IS COMPRESSED THROUGH HERE.

FUEL INJECTOR

FUEL IS IGNITED AND COMBINED WITH COMPRESSED AIR.

The IGNITED FUEL/ COMPRESSED AIR COMBO PRODUCES HOT, EXPANDING GASES.

THESE SAME EXPANDING GASES SPIN THE TURBINE.

HIGH-SPEED, HOT AIR IS EXPELLED, PRODUCING THRUST!

Fighter Jet Blueprint

This is an F-16 Fighting Falcon. It's a formidable weapon and one of the backbones of the United States military arsenal, so it's a good example to use for a basic fighter blueprint.

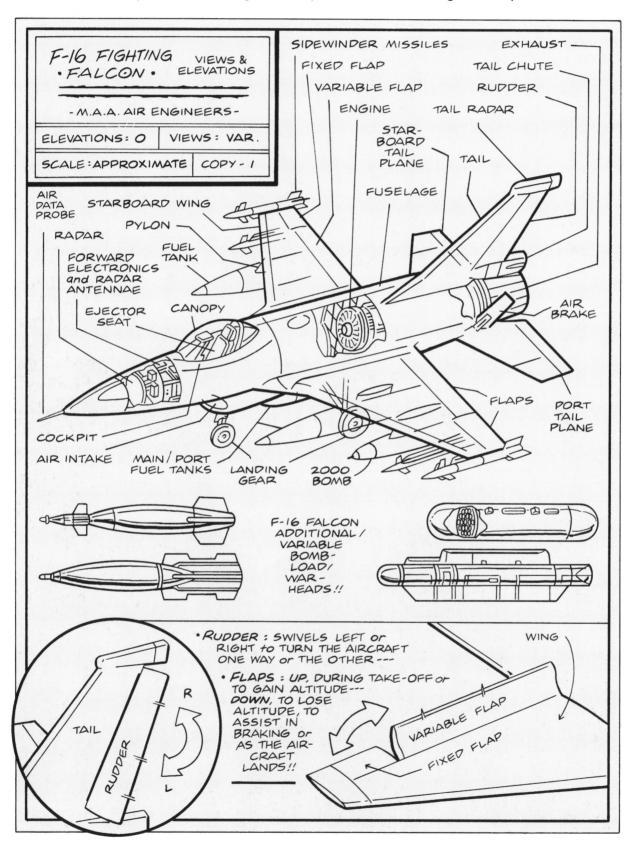

F-16 FIGHTING • FALCON •   VIEWS & ELEVATIONS

- M.A.A. AIR ENGINEERS -

ELEVATIONS: O | VIEWS: VAR.

SCALE: APPROXIMATE | COPY - 1

SIDEWINDER MISSILES
FIXED FLAP
VARIABLE FLAP
ENGINE
STAR-BOARD TAIL PLANE
FUSELAGE
EXHAUST
TAIL CHUTE
RUDDER
TAIL RADAR
TAIL
AIR BRAKE
PORT TAIL PLANE
FLAPS

AIR DATA PROBE
STARBOARD WING
PYLON
RADAR
FUEL TANK
FORWARD ELECTRONICS and RADAR ANTENNAE
EJECTOR SEAT
CANOPY
COCKPIT
AIR INTAKE
MAIN / PORT FUEL TANKS
LANDING GEAR
2000 BOMB

F-16 FALCON ADDITIONAL / VARIABLE BOMB- LOAD/ WAR- HEADS!!

• RUDDER : SWIVELS LEFT or RIGHT to TURN THE AIRCRAFT ONE WAY or THE OTHER ---

• FLAPS : UP, DURING TAKE-OFF or TO GAIN ALTITUDE --- DOWN, TO LOSE ALTITUDE, TO ASSIST IN BRAKING or AS THE AIR- CRAFT LANDS!!

WING
VARIABLE FLAP
FIXED FLAP

TAIL
RUDDER
R
L

F-16 Fighting Falcon

A major component of the nation's air force, the F-16 is a tough, compact, multirole fighter designed for both air-to-air combat and air-to-surface attacks. It was used successfully in Operation Desert Storm during the Persian Gulf War. Loaded with devastating sidewinder missiles, a 20mm multibarrel cannon wielding 500 rounds, and an advanced radar system, it seeks out and destroys the enemy in broad daylight, cover of night, or any kind of weather. It climbs to a maximum altitude of over 50,000 feet, has a top speed of 1,500 mph (which is Mach 2, or twice the speed of sound), and can fly 2,000 miles on a single mission. Admired for its maneuverability and speed, it can also fly over 500 miles without refueling. Makes its $20 million price tag seem like a bargain!

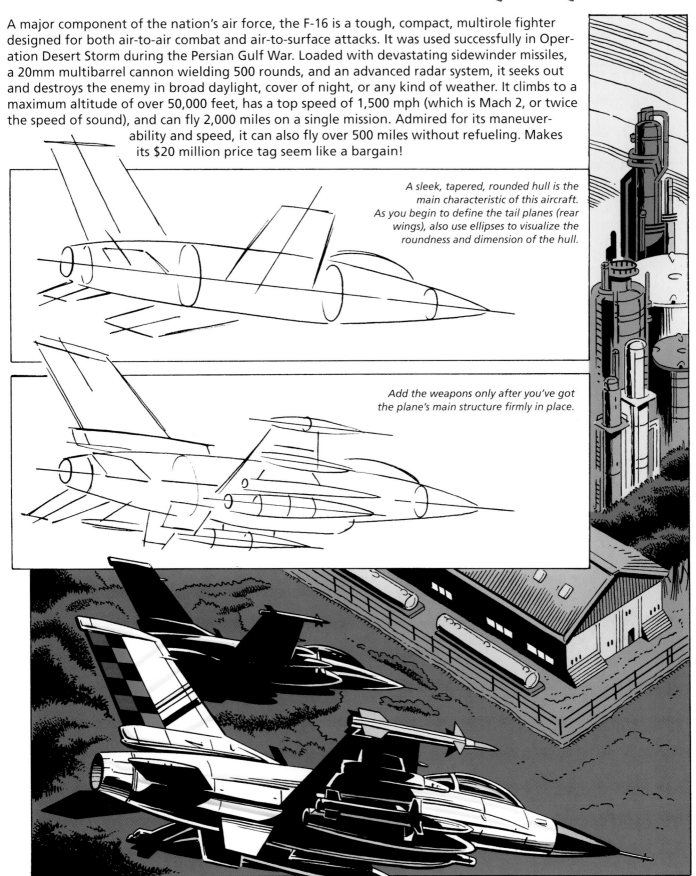

A sleek, tapered, rounded hull is the main characteristic of this aircraft. As you begin to define the tail planes (rear wings), also use ellipses to visualize the roundness and dimension of the hull.

Add the weapons only after you've got the plane's main structure firmly in place.

F-117A Nighthawk Stealth Fighter

The world's first aircraft designed to exploit low-observable stealth technology, the Stealth bomber is the ultimate high-tech war weapon. Its body design makes it invisible to enemy radar.

When drawing this plane, think *angles*. Unlike other aircraft, which have a rounded shape to improve aerodynamics, the Stealth is made up completely of flat surfaces and sharp edges. This enables it to avoid radar detection. It works like this: The radar antenna sends out a signal that's reflected back to it by any object it encounters. By measuring the time it takes to receive a returned signal, you can tell how far away the object is. Rounded surfaces will always reflect some of a radar signal back to its source, no matter where the signal hits the plane—and it will be enough to register as a large object. Flat surfaces, however, will reflect the radar signal away at an angle, rather than back to the signal's originating point. As a result, most Stealth-reflected radar signals don't make it back to the transmission point.

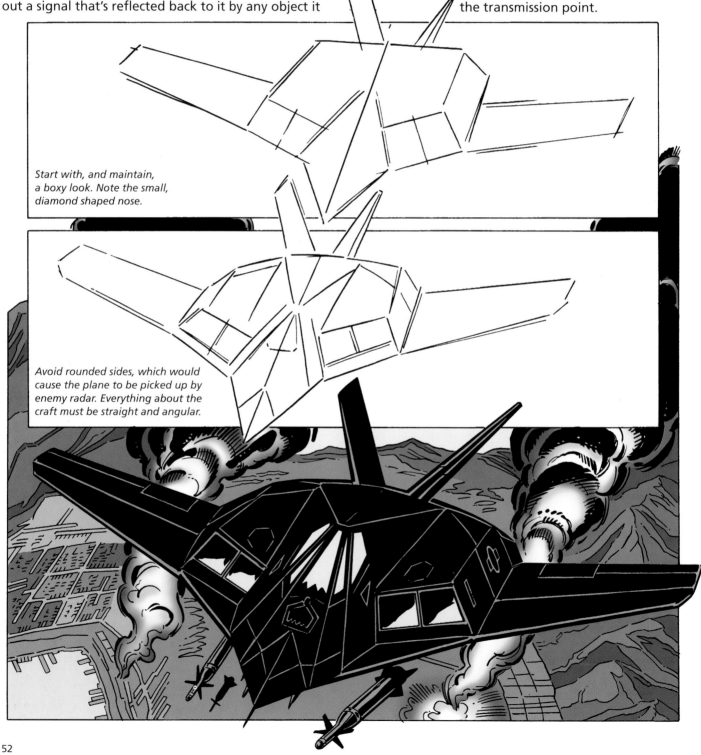

Start with, and maintain, a boxy look. Note the small, diamond shaped nose.

Avoid rounded sides, which would cause the plane to be picked up by enemy radar. Everything about the craft must be straight and angular.

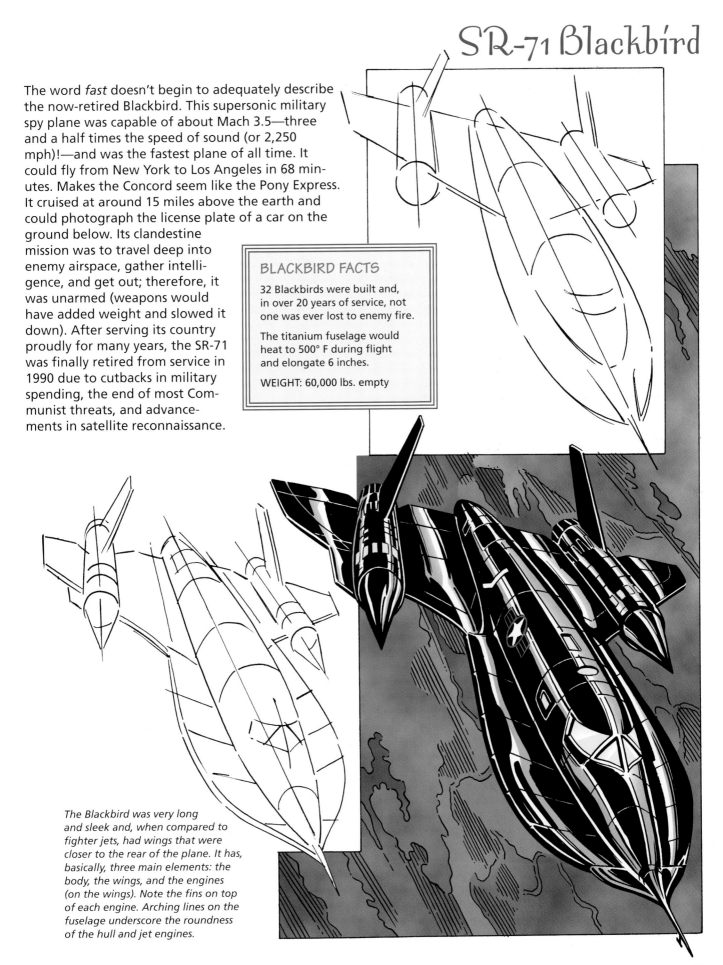

SR-71 Blackbird

The word *fast* doesn't begin to adequately describe the now-retired Blackbird. This supersonic military spy plane was capable of about Mach 3.5—three and a half times the speed of sound (or 2,250 mph)!—and was the fastest plane of all time. It could fly from New York to Los Angeles in 68 minutes. Makes the Concord seem like the Pony Express. It cruised at around 15 miles above the earth and could photograph the license plate of a car on the ground below. Its clandestine mission was to travel deep into enemy airspace, gather intelligence, and get out; therefore, it was unarmed (weapons would have added weight and slowed it down). After serving its country proudly for many years, the SR-71 was finally retired from service in 1990 due to cutbacks in military spending, the end of most Communist threats, and advancements in satellite reconnaissance.

BLACKBIRD FACTS

32 Blackbirds were built and, in over 20 years of service, not one was ever lost to enemy fire.

The titanium fuselage would heat to 500° F during flight and elongate 6 inches.

WEIGHT: 60,000 lbs. empty

The Blackbird was very long and sleek and, when compared to fighter jets, had wings that were closer to the rear of the plane. It has, basically, three main elements: the body, the wings, and the engines (on the wings). Note the fins on top of each engine. Arching lines on the fuselage underscore the roundness of the hull and jet engines.

Tornado

The Tornado began as a team effort between England, Italy, and Germany. It's a twin-seater, multirole aircraft—for both ground attack and air defense—that reaches a maximum speed of about Mach 2. It possesses significant firepower, including Mauser cannons, laser-guided missiles, HARMs (high-speed antiradiation missiles), radar decoys, and free-falling bombs.

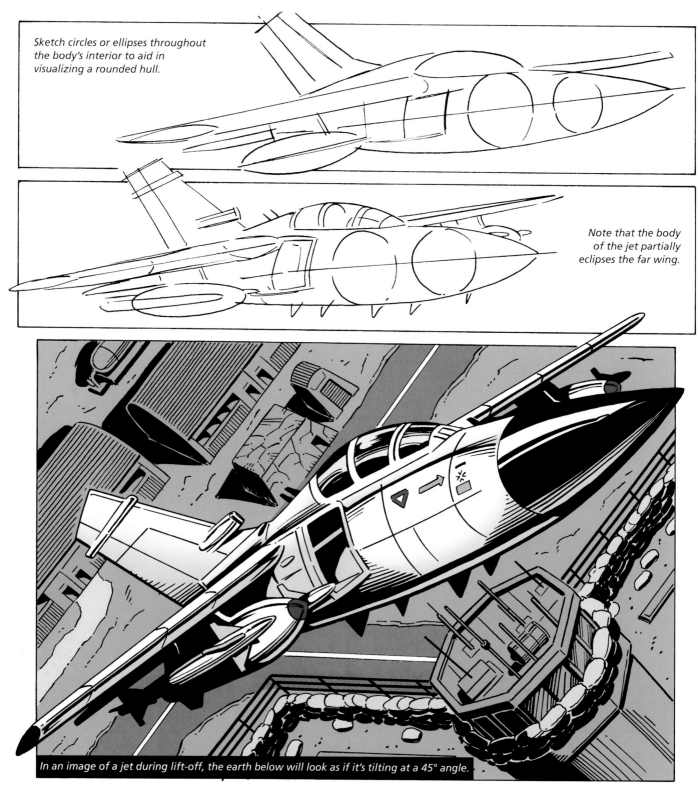

Sketch circles or ellipses throughout the body's interior to aid in visualizing a rounded hull.

Note that the body of the jet partially eclipses the far wing.

In an image of a jet during lift-off, the earth below will look as if it's tilting at a 45° angle.

F-22 Raptor

A raptor is a bird of prey, and it's no coincidence that this supersonic jet is named after it. Capable of Mach 1.8 (Mach 1.5 at supercruise, explained below), and with a reported cost of $95 million per jet, this indomitable flying arsenal has incredible acceleration powers and can fly amazing distances. It's the first aircraft to possess supercruise capability, which is the ability to cruise at supersonic speeds without the use of the fuel-consuming afterburners that other aircraft rely on for extended high-speed flight. This means that the Raptor can get to the battle faster and remain in combat longer than other fighters without expending its fuel supply. Due to new technology, the Raptor allows its pilot to see the enemy sooner and fire before they know

what hit 'em. Stocked with a variety of medium and short-range missiles, plus stealth technology, the F-22 performs magnificently in both air-to-air and air-to-surface combat.

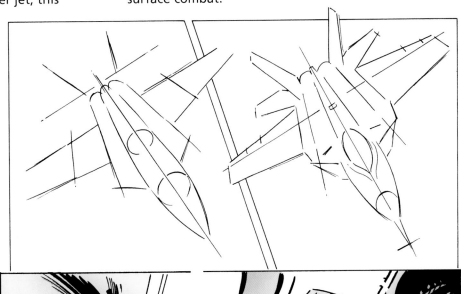

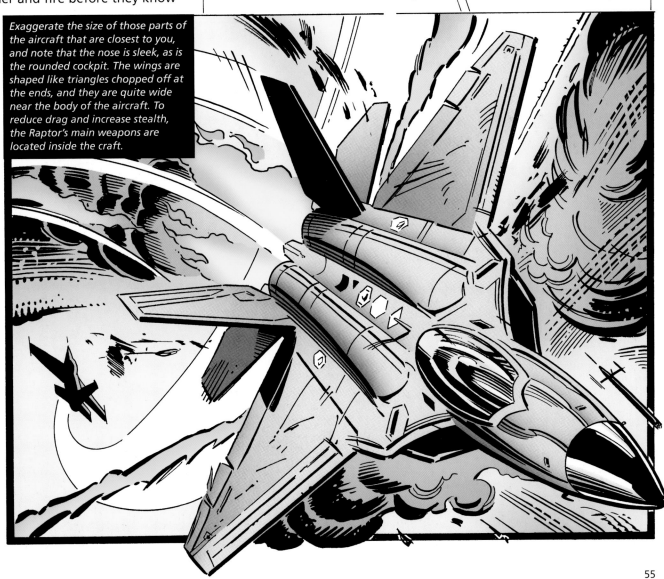

Exaggerate the size of those parts of the aircraft that are closest to you, and note that the nose is sleek, as is the rounded cockpit. The wings are shaped like triangles chopped off at the ends, and they are quite wide near the body of the aircraft. To reduce drag and increase stealth, the Raptor's main weapons are located inside the craft.

MiG-29 Fulcrum

This Russian fighter jet has earned respect from aviation experts. Built to engage the American F-16 Fighting Falcon in air combat, it's a multirole aircraft, capable of air-to-air and air-to-surface combat, and also used for escorting other aircraft. Made of aluminum-lithium alloy, it's a single-pilot fighter capable of reaching speeds of Mach 2.3, although it's reported to be less maneuverable than the F-16 at velocities above the speed of sound.

When you start, always sketch the wings as a single line uninterrupted by the fuselage (the body). Then erase these guidelines later. Note the descended wheels as the plane lands.

The double-tail fins and twin exhausts are signature features of the MiG.

A-10 Thunderbolt

The Thunderbolt is an enemy tank's worst nightmare. It was one of the first Air Force crafts to be specifically designed for close air support of ground targets, and its aluminum frame allows it to maneuver at low altitudes to hunt down ground targets. The titanium-enclosed cockpit protects the pilots from enemy fire. Equipped with NVIS (Night Vision Imaging Systems) and night-vision goggles, the Thunderbolt can strike at night, when visibility is poor. It can fire up to 3,900 rounds per minute and carries a formidable array of missiles with it. Nicknamed "the Warthog" for both its tank-busting abilities and its ugly appearance, it's still a beauty in battle. The cost: mere pocket change at only about $9 million per aircraft.

The tail plane (rear wing) is wide, with fins that stick up on each end.

The two large, twin-engines are mounted behind the wings.

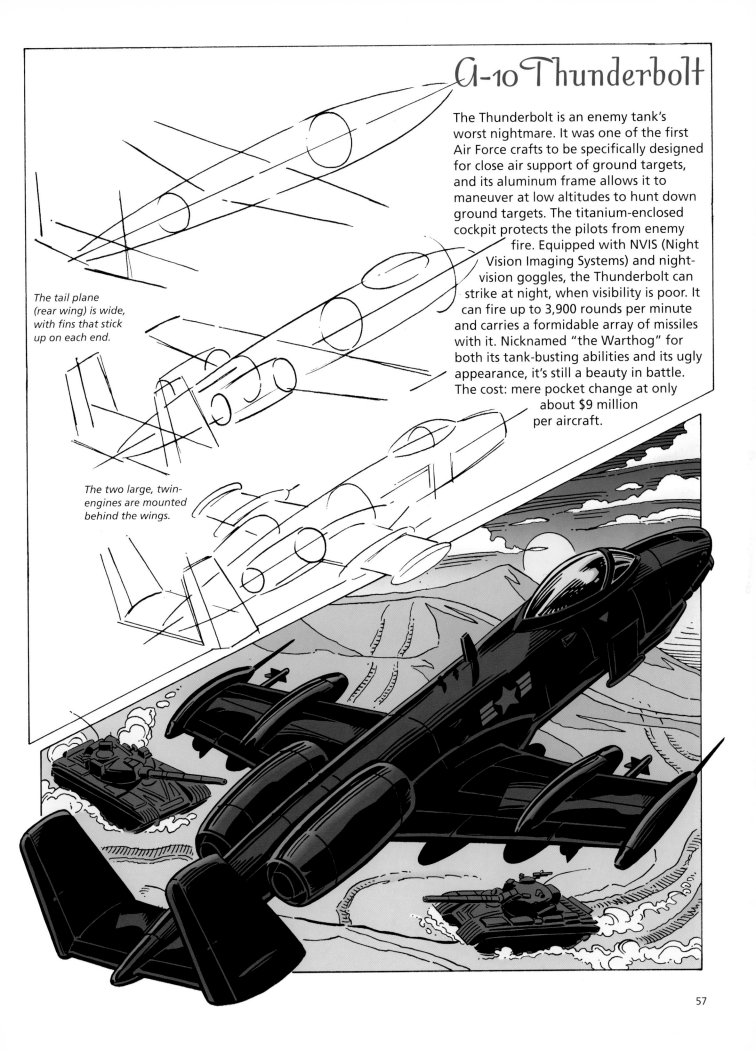

GH-64D Apache Longbow Attack Helicopter

You may think a helicopter isn't as awesome a weapon as a fighter jet, but underestimating the Apache Longbow could be a deadly mistake. It's a twin-engine chopper that's radar equipped, with night vision, and can fire up to 625 rounds per minute. That's one round every .096 seconds! Try dodging them bullets. In the Persian Gulf War, Apaches took out over 500 enemy tanks.

The Apache Longbow is also loaded with over 70 rockets and 16 laser-guided Longbow Hellfire missiles. (Hellfire stands for HELicopter-Launched FIRE-and-forget.) Through a digitized target acquisition system, the Longbow can automatically simultaneously detect and classify over 128 targets, identify the 16 most dangerous, transmit that information to other Apaches, and attack—all within 30 seconds of initiation of radar scan.

Note that the Apache isn't drawn with the rounded lines and curves you'd expect to find on a civilian helicopter or aircraft, but with almost exclusively straight lines and angles. (Compare with the helicopter on page 25.)

H.O.T.A.S. - HANDS ON THROTTLE and STICK - Detail.

ATTACK COMMIT BUTTON

REVISIONARY TRIMMER —

ATTACK MODES SELECTOR

NOSE-WHEEL STEER-ING DIS-ENGAGE

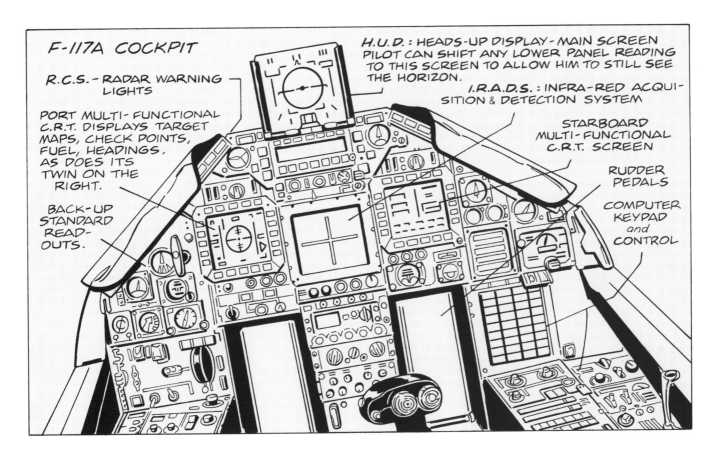

F-117A COCKPIT

R.C.S. – RADAR WARNING LIGHTS

PORT MULTI-FUNCTIONAL C.R.T. DISPLAYS TARGET MAPS, CHECK POINTS, FUEL, HEADINGS, AS DOES ITS TWIN ON THE RIGHT.

BACK-UP STANDARD READ-OUTS.

H.U.D.: HEADS-UP DISPLAY – MAIN SCREEN PILOT CAN SHIFT ANY LOWER PANEL READING TO THIS SCREEN TO ALLOW HIM TO STILL SEE THE HORIZON.

I.R.A.D.S.: INFRA-RED ACQUI-SITION & DETECTION SYSTEM

STARBOARD MULTI-FUNCTIONAL C.R.T. SCREEN

RUDDER PEDALS

COMPUTER KEYPAD and CONTROL

L-39C Albatross Jet Trainer

Used in the United States strictly for schooling young pilots in the art of flying combat missions, the L-39C Albatross is referred to as a "trainer" aircraft. It seats two crew members in tandem, maxes out at a speed of 469 mph, and has only 2½ hours of fuel available per tank. Once purchased by the United States, these reliable, foreign-built jet trainers are inspected and retooled to conform to Federal Aviation Administration (FAA) standards.

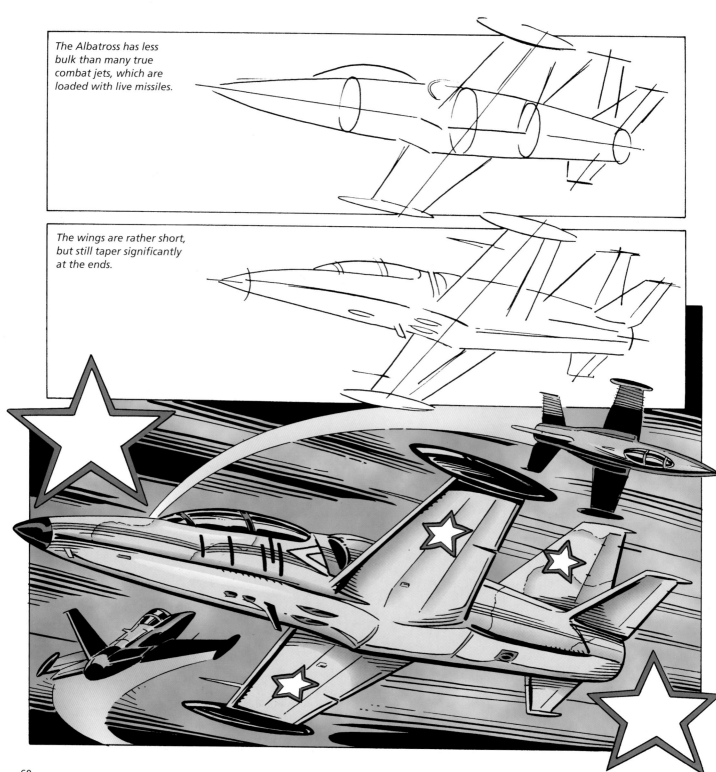

The Albatross has less bulk than many true combat jets, which are loaded with live missiles.

The wings are rather short, but still taper significantly at the ends.

Fighter Plane Nose Designs

Fighter pilots put their lives on the line every time they enter a cockpit. They rely on their jets, which are more than a tool; they're a partner. If pilots have a mission, then so do their jets. Many jets are painted with designs that reflect their function. Some display birds of prey, for example. Others sport bared teeth, cobras, skulls and crossbones, or charging animals. Still for others, just showing the good old stars and stripes says it all.

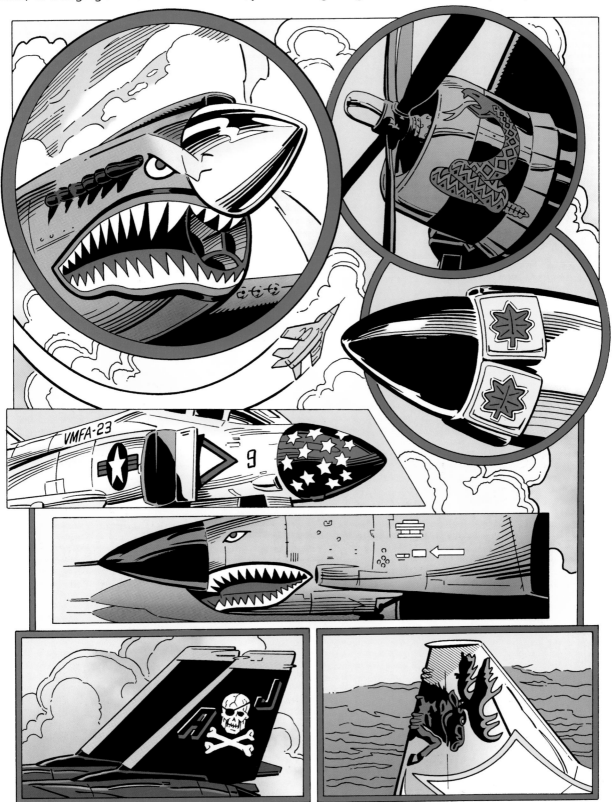

AWACS Radar Plane

The AWACS (Airborne Warning and Control System) plane doesn't shoot down enemies from the sky or even target missile sites on the ground, but that doesn't mean it's not essential to the nation's air defenses. It is designed to locate targets miles away and relay that information to fighter pilots who can then move in and take out the enemy. It does its job at high altitudes, out of range of SAMS (surface-to-air missiles).

AWACS radar can separate airborne targets from the ground and sea clutter that confuses other radars, and it can detect and track both air and sea targets simultaneously. Its radar "eye" has a 360° view of the horizon, and it can "see" more than 200 miles away. In addition, this radar technology is always being upgraded to stay two steps ahead of the enemy.

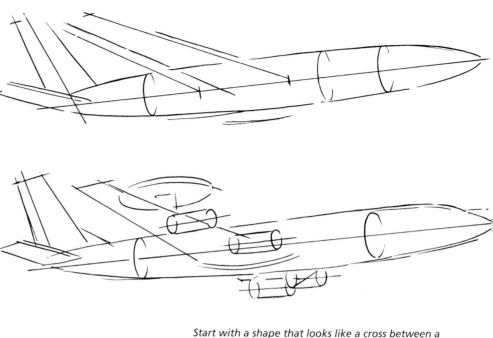

Start with a shape that looks like a cross between a fighter jet and a passenger airliner. And remember: Those are engines underneath the wings—not missiles—so don't make them pointed, as you would for weapons.

R2-3A "DarkStar" Tier III Minus

No longer in use, this elegant, futuristic aircraft was a UAV (Unmanned Aerial Vehicle). Nicknamed the DarkStar, it needed no pilot and was preprogrammed to serve its function: continuous, all-weather, wide-area reconnaissance—in highly defended areas—in support of tactical commanders. It was extremely light at only 8,600 lbs. and had such advanced stealth technology that it could penetrate deep into enemy territory unseen. However, like many promising undertakings, DarkStar production was canceled in early 1999 due to budget cuts and some demands that even it couldn't handle.

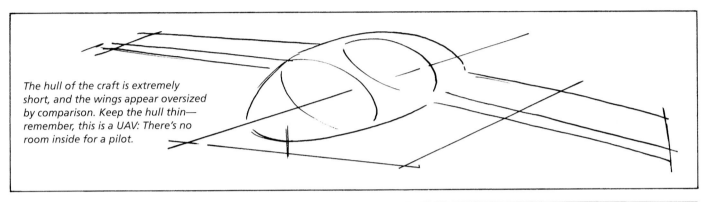

The hull of the craft is extremely short, and the wings appear oversized by comparison. Keep the hull thin— remember, this is a UAV: There's no room inside for a pilot.

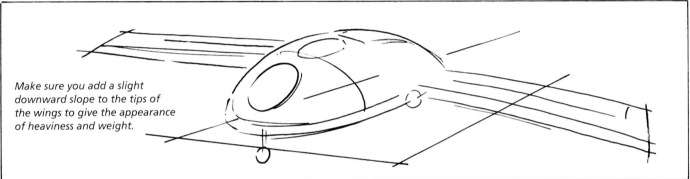

Make sure you add a slight downward slope to the tips of the wings to give the appearance of heaviness and weight.

INDEX

accidents, race car, 37
aircraft
    AWACS (Airborne Warning and Control System) radar plane, 62
    early machines, 46–47
    passenger jet, 9
    propeller, 48
    R2-3A "DarkStar" Tier 111 Minus, 63
    SR-71 Blackbird spy plane, 53
    see also fighter jets; helicopters
Albatross jet trainer, 60
Alfa Romeo, 15
angles, 20–21
    fighter jet, 52
    3/4 view, 33, 40–41
Apache Longbow Attack Helicopter, 58–59
assembly line, 6
Aston Martin DB5, 30
A-10 Thunderbolt, 57
AWACS (Airborne Warning and Control System) radar plane, 62

Blackbird spy plane, 53
BMW 507, 28
bombs, 50, 54
Bond, James
    Aston Martin DB5, 30
    Lotus Esprit, 17
braking system, 11
Bugatti Atlantic, 26
Bugatti, Ettore, 26

car chase
    from air, 25
    police car, 24
cars
    basic shapes, 8–9
    blueprint, 10–11
    crushed by monster trucks, 42–45
    engine, 12
    history of, 6
    wheels, 13
    see also classic car; race car; sports car
Charger, 21
chassis
    generic sedan, 10–11
    monster truck, 45
Chevrolet Corvette, 21
classic car
    Aston Martin DB5, 30
    BMW 507, 28
    Bugatti Atlantic, 26
    Jaguar E-Type, 29
    Lamborghini Miura, 31
    Mercedes-Benz 300 SL "Gullwing" Coupe, 27
cockpit
    A-10 Thunderbolt, 57
    Apache Longbow Attack Helicopter, 59
    blueprint, 50
Corvette, 21
crowd scenes, 36

"DarkStar" Tier 111 Minus, 63
detailing, 43
Dodge
    Charger, 21
    Viper GTS Coupe, 19, 20

engine
    car, 10, 12
    jet, 48, 49

Falcon fighter jet, 50, 51, 56
Ferrari, Enzo, 15
Ferrari
    F 50, 15
    F 355, 20
fighter jets
    A-10 Thunderbolt, 57
    blueprint, 50
    engine, 48, 49
    F-117A Nighthawk Stealth, 52
    F-16 Falcon, 50, 51
    F-22 Raptor, 55
    L-39C Albatross trainer, 60
    MiG-29 Fulcrum, 56
    nose designs, 61
    Tornado, 54
fighter plane, propeller, 48
F-117A Nighthawk Stealth fighter, 52
Ford, Henry, 6
Ford Mustang, 21, 22–23, 25
Formula One car, 32
4-stroke combustion cycle, 12
F-16 Fighting Falcon, 50, 51, 56
F-22 Raptor, 55

Goldfinger, 30
gullwing doors, 16, 27

HARMS (high-speed antiradiation missiles), 54
helicopters
    Apache Longbow Attack Helicopter, 58–59
    in car chase, 25
H.O.T.A.S (hands on throttle and stick), 58
hubcaps, 13

Jaguar E-Type, 29
jets. See aircraft; fighter jets

Lamborghini
    Countach, 16
    Diablo, 20
    Miura, 31
Le Mans race car, 33
Lotus Esprit, 17
L-39C Albatross trainer, 60

Mach speeds, 51, 53, 54, 55, 56
Mauser cannons, 54
Mercedes-Benz 300 SL "Gullwing" Coupe, 27
MiG-29 Fulcrum, 56
missiles, 55
    HARMS (high-speed antiradiation), 54
    laser-guided, 54
    Longbow Hellfire, 58
    sidewinder, 51
multiple-cylinder engines, 12
muscle cars, 21
Mustang, 21, 22–23, 25

NVIS (Night Vision Imaging Systems), 57

Operation Desert Storm.
    See Persian Gulf War

paint job
    fighter jets, 61
    trucks, 43
Persian Gulf War
    Apache Longbow Attack Helicopter, 58–59
    F-16 Fighting Falcon, 51
perspective, 8, 14
pit crew, 36
police car, 24
Pontiac Firebird Trans Am, 21
Porsche 911 Turbo, 18, 20
propeller planes, 48

race car
    accidents, 37
    Formula One, 32
    Le Mans, 33
    pit crew, 36
    rally cross, 35
    stock car, 34, 36
    wheels, 13
radar, AWACS, 62
radar antenna, 52
rally cross race car, 35
Raptor fighter jet, 55
rudder, fighter jet, 50
Russian fighter jet, MiG-29 Fulcrum, 56

sidewinder missiles, 51
sports car
    angles, 20
    basic shape, 9
    Corvette, 21
    Dodge Charger, 21
    Dodge Viper GTS Coupe, 19, 20
    Ferrari F 50, 15
    Ferrari F 355, 20
    Ford Mustang, 21, 22–23
    generic, 14
    Lamborghini Countach, 16
    Lamborghini Diablo, 20
    Lotus Esprit, 17
    Porsche 911 Turbo, 18, 20
    Trans Am, 21
spy plane, 53
Spy Who Loved Me, The, 17
stealth
    F-117A Nighthawk fighter, 52
    R2-3A "DarkStar" Tier 111 Minus, 63
stock car, 34
    pit crew, 36
supercruise capability, 55

3/4 views, 33, 40–41
Thunderball, 30
Thunderbolt fighter jet, 57
tires, 8, 13, 41
Tornado fighter jet, 54
Trans Am, 21
trucks, monster, 38–39
    basic shape, 9
    chassis, 45
    crushing cars, 42–45
    paint jobs, 43
    3/4 views, 40–41
    wheels, 13, 41

UAV (Unmanned Aerial Vehicle), 63

vanishing lines, 8, 32
vanishing point, 8

war heads, 50
wheelbase, 10
wheels, 8, 13, 41
wings, fighter jet, 50, 53, 56